VIGYAN BHAIRAVA TANTRA

A Science of Concentration and Meditation

MOHAN KUMAR
(AUTHOR)

THANKFULNESS

Thank you to those who read my first book and gave me the courage and the belief that I could really do this.

Thank you to those who purchased my books and recommend it to their friends and continue to spread the words.

Thank you to everyone who showed up for my first book signing to show your support.

Thank you to everyone who has taken time out of their day to read it.

Thank you tp everyone who has reviewed my book and sent me honest kind words. There is no greater gift to an author and it means more than you know.

And, the most important thank you... THANK YOU to my parents, my friends and every single one of you who have supported me from day one. You have inspired me to continue to go after dreams. You have brightened dark days. You helped me to believe that I can do anything I set my mind to and you have helped me achieve what I once thought was impossible.

For that and for all of you – I will be forever grateful.

3

INTRODUCTION

After getting love and positive response of my previous book "Shiv Swarodaya – A Divine Law of Breathing" and "The Basic Mantras", of the series " The Mantras" ; now, I am presenting a new book on meditation "Vigyan Bhairav Tantra" (Edition 2) to boost and take your spiritual and meditation level in zenith. Recently, I also wrote book namely, "Black Magic & Witchcraft " which will help you in your daily life in many ways.

The "Vigyan Bhairav Tantra" is an ancient Indian text book of around 5,000 years old which is considered by many as the only book of meditation. This book is originally in Sanskrit. The book, which is before you, is the exact translation of the original text book.

No discussion is complete on meditation without mentioning this book. It contains 112 methods and techniques of meditation in the form of conversation between God Shiva and Goddess Parvati (Devi, Gazelle-eyed). Many Sadhus, Saints, Gurus, etc. are also using these techniques of meditation.

The book "Vigyan Bhairava Tantra" literally means : Bhairava – A God of Hindu religion or another name of God Shiva; Tantra – A mystical spiritual path, a specific ancient science; Science – Vigyan. In this book, 112 techniques of meditation are discussed which can also help you for realizing your own true self.

The book "Vigyan Bhairav Tantra" is started with conversation between God Shiva and Goddesss Parvati (Shakti). Devi asked God Shiva about the nature of reality, about

Universe, about fundamental nature of the world. She also asked God Shiva, how can one go beyond space and time to understand this truth. God Shiva does not answer her directly of her questions. Rather than he tells her about the methods and techniques to get answers of these questions. He tells her how one can realize this reality through 112 methods of entering in the self. As every person has his own specific problems and questions. This book not only helped Goddess Parvati to get her answers but also can help same to the entire world.

The methods are in their seed form which points towards various powerful meditation and concentration techniques. On contemplating about these techniques, you will get one of the most powerful collections of meditation techniques which are simple and very effective.

The Book "Vigyan Bhairav Tantra" has 112 meditation methods and techniques which covered all meditation techniques and methods. These meditational techniques and methods can be used by the people of all ages and times (past, present and future).

It is impossible to find a meditational method or technique beyond these 112 techniques. It is also impossible for anybody to find a technique which is not suitable to his own level of spiritual development and inner temperament.

SHRI DEVI SAID :

O Dev ! I have listened all in detail that
has emerged from Rudrayamala
Tantra. I have also understood Trika,
the three divisions of shakti, which is
the essence or secret of all knowledge.

O Supreme God ! Inspite of everything
that I have listened, even till now my
doubts are not clear. O Lord ! What is
your reality? Are you the energy that
contained in sound from which all the
mantras have originated?

9

Can your reality be known by the nine ways from which one can enter the zone of higher consciousness, as revealed by Bhairav in Bhairava Tantra? Is it different from the procedure in Trishira Bhairav Tantra? Can it be known by the knowledge of the triple forms of Shakti (power), i.e. Para, Parapara, and Apara?

Is it Nada or Bindu or can it be known by concentrating on the ascending psychic centres or the unstruck sound which emerge without any vibration? Or is it the form of the obstructing half moon or else is it the form of shakti?

Is your reality transcendent and immanent or is it completely immanent or completely transcendental? If it is immanent then the very nature of transcendence is contradicted.

Transcendence can not exist in the divisions of colour, sound or form. If transcendence is indivisible, then it can not be defined with composite parts. O Lord ! Please, clear my all doubts completely.

LORD BHAIRAVA SAID :

O Dear ! Good – Good, well said. What you have asked about is the essence of Tantra.

11

O Devi ! Although this is the most secret part of the Tantras. Now, I will speak to you that has explained about the forms of Bhairava.

O Devi ! The shakra aspect of Bhirava is unreal and of no spiritual value, like the illusory dream and like the delusion of celestial musicians.

All Sadhanas are described for those who deluded intellect, who are victim to distracted thought patterns or are inclined towards the performance of action and ostentatious rituals to traverse the path of meditation.

In reality, the essence of Bhairava is not the nine forms, nor the garland of letters, nor the three flows and not even the three energies of Shakti (power).

Bhairava can not be known in nada and bindu not even in the obstructed half moon, not in the piercing of successive chakras, not power or energy constitute his essence.

These things have been said like the tales to frighten children, to induce person of immature intellect to follow the spiritual path, just as the mother entices her child with sweets.

The form of Bhairava can not be measured in terms of time, space or direction, nor can it be indicated by any attribute or designation.

One can have this inner experience for oneself when the mind is free from modifications or thought patterns. The soul of Bhairava, which is known as Bhairavi, is then experienced as the bliss of one's own inner awareness, a state whose form is fullness, free from all contradictations.

The essence of his nature is known to be free of dross and pervades the entire universe. This being the nature of the highest reality, who is the object of worship and who is to be pacified by worship?

In this way the transcendental state of Bhairava, which is described is known by means of the absolute of highest form that is Paradevi, the supreme Goddess.

Just like, Shakti (power) is not different from mighty (the holder of power), similarly Parashakti (the supreme power), can never be separated from Bhairava.

Just like, the power of burning is not different from fire, similarly Parashakti is not different from Bhairava. However, it is assumed as different in the beginning, in a primary stage towards entry into its knowledge.

One who enters the state of Shakti (power), has the feeling of identification with Shiva, without division. Then one may become like the form of Shiva i.e. Shakti is the face of Lord Shiva.

Just like, form, space and direction are revealed by the flame of a Dipak or the sun, similarly Shiva is revealed by the medium of Shakti.

SHRI DEVI SAID :

O God of Gods ! , who bears the trident and skulls as ornaments, tell me of that state which is devoid of time, space and direction and free from any characteristics.

By what means can that state of fullness of Bhairava be achieved, and how does Paradevi, the highest power, become the face or entrance of Bhairava? O Bhairava ! Tell me in the manner, so that I shall know it completely.

SHRI BHAIRAVA SAID :

Paradevi, whose nature is Visarga (creation), manifests as the upward prana (inhale breath) and the downward apana (exhale breath). By concentrating the mind at the two points of generation of prana and apana, the state of fullness achieved.

When the ingoing pranic air (inhale breath) and outgoing pranic air (exhale breath) are both restrained in their space from their (respective points of) return, the essence of Bhairava, which is not different from Bhairavi, manifests.

When Shakti (power) in the form of air or breath (vayu) is still and does not flow swiftly in a specific direction, there develops in the middle, through the state of Nirvikalp, the form of Bhairava.

When Kumbhaka takes place after Puraka or Rechaka, then the Shakti as peace is experienced and by that peace, the Bhairava i.e. conciousness is revealed.

Concentrate on the Shakti (energy) arising from the root like the rays of the sun, gradually becoming subtle and subtler, until at last it dissolves in the dwadashanta and Bhairava manifests.

Concentrate on the Shakti which is moving upwards like lightning through which all the chakras moving one by one to the dwadashanta. Then at last the glorious form of Bhairava dawns.

The twelve centres in a series should be pierced successively through proper understanding of their twelve letters. Thus, becoming liberated from the gross then the subtle, one by one, at the end of its journey the Kundalini becomes Shiva.

Then, having filled the tip of moordha (forehead) and crossed the bridge between the eyebrows, the mind rises above all dichotomizing thought patterns and omnipresence.

Like different coloured circles on the peacock's feathers, one should concentrate on the five voids. Then by following them to the end, which

21

becomes the priciple void, enter the heart.

In this way, wherever there is mindful awareness, either on the void, or on another object, or on a noble person like Guru, gradually the boon of absorption into the self is granted.

By closing eyes, and focusing at the centre of the forehead, gradually, the mind stabilizes and direct it towards the goal, which will become distinguishable and clear.

One should concentrate on the inner space of the medial Nadi (Sushuman Nadi) situated in the central axis of the body (spinal cord) which is as slender as a fibre of the lotus stem, and then by the grace of Devi, the divine form of Bhairava is revealed.

By using the hands as tools to block the entrances in all directions, the eyebrow centre is pierced and bindu (light) is seen. Being gradually absorbed within that, the supreme state Bhairava is realised.

Whenever one concentrate upon the subtle lire, in the form of a Tilak (a mark worn by a Hindu on the forehead

23

as an ornament), or on the Bindu at the end of the shikha, a condition of agitation and shaking is produced, followed by absorption and dissolution in the core of heart.

One who is adept in listening to the unstruck sound in anahata, which is uninterrupted like a rushing river, attains the supreme state of Brahma by mastery of Shabdabrahaman, the form of Brahman as sound.

One who repeats the Pranava (OM) perfectly, while concentrating on the void for protracted periods, experiences the void, and by that void the transcendental shakti, the Bhairava is revealed.

Whoever contemplates even on the maatras or letters (of OM) from first to last, in the form of void, verily that Sadhaka by concentrating on the void becomes the void.

When one pointed awareness on the prolonged inner sounds of different musical instruments, like stringed, wind and percussion, is gradually established, in the end the body becomes the supreme space.

By repetition of all the gross letters of the bija mantras successively, including the sound 'M', and concentrating on the void within each sound, one verily becomes Shiva.

All the directions should be contemplated upon simultaneously in one's own body as space or void. The mind too being free from all thoughts becomes dissolved in the vacuous space of consciousness.

One who contemplates simultaneously on the void of the back (spinal cord) and the void of the root becomes void minded (completely free from all thoughts which contructs by that energy which is independent of the body.

By steady contemplation on the void of the back (Sushumna), the void of the root and the void of the heart simultaneously, there arises the state of Nirvikalpa, which ir free from all thoughts which constructs.

If one concentrates on the body as a void, even for a moment, with the mind free from thought, then one attains thoughtlessness and verily becomes that form of void, then the Bhairava revealed.

O gazelle eyed ! One when concentrate upon all the constituents of the body pervaded by space, so that that thought becomes steady.

One should contemplate on the skin of the body as a mere wall or partition with nothing inside it. By concentrating, he becomes like the void, which can not be concentrated upon.

O embodiment of good fortune, one who contemplates with closed eyes and one pointed concentration on the mantra in the middle of the lotus in the

heart space achieves the highest
spiritual realisation.

When the mind is dissolved in
dwadashanta by steady awareness and
steady practice, the true nature or
essence of the goal manifests
everywhere in one's body.

By bringing the mind forcibly to
dwadashanta again and again,
however and wherever possible, the
fluctuations of the mind diminish day
by day, so that each moment becomes
an extraordinary state.

One should contemplate that one's own body has been burnt by Kaalagni, arising, form the movement of time. Then at last one will experience tranquility.

In the same way, concentrating with an unwavering and one pointed mind on the entire universe being burnt by Kaalagni, that man becomes a godman or attains a supreme state of manhood.

Dharana (beliefs) on those constituents which comprise one's own body and the whole universe, such as the tattwas ans tanmantras, from subtle to subtlest, leads to the source of existence. In this way, Paradevi (the almighty Goddess), is revealed at the end of meditation.

If you meditate on the gross and weak Shakti (energy) in the twelve Indriyas (sense organs), thus making it subtle, one who enters the heart space and meditate there attains mukti (final beatitude) and becomes liberated.

By concentrating on the entire form of the universe and the course of its development through time and space, gradually dissolve the gross into the subtle and the subtle into the state of being beyond, until the mind is finally dissolved into pure conciousness.

31

By this method one should concentrate on all the sides or aspects of the universe up to the Shiva Tatva (which is quintessence) of all. Thus, the experience of the supreme reality arises and Bhairava revealed.

O Great Goddess ! One should concentrate on this universe as nothing but void. Dissolving the mind, one then experiences the Laya state, or total disintegration.

One should concentrate or fix his sight (on the empty space) inside the pot,

32

leaving aside the enclosing struture. Thus, the pot will be vanished, the mind will at once be disintegrated into the space. Through that Laya (penetration, rhythm) the mind becomes completely absorbed into the void.

One should fix or concentrate his sight or gaze on a treeless place, like bare mountains or rocks, where there is no support for the mind to dwell on. Then the modification of the mind become less and the experience of dissolution takes place.

One should think of two objects, and in the event of such knowledge being

33

matured, then cast both aside and dwell on the gap or space in the middle. On conecentrating in the middle, the experience of the essence arises.

When the mind is restrained to one object of awareness, casting all others aside and not allowing movement to take place from one to another, then inside that perception the awareness thrives.

One should concentrate with an unwavering mind on all existence, the body and even the universe simultaneoulsy as nothing but conciousness, then the supreme consciousness arises and then the Bhairava revealed.

From the fusion of both Vayus (Prana and Apana) inside or outside (the body), the yogi attains equilibrium and becomes fir for the proper manifestation of consciousness.

One should contemplate simultaneously on the entire universe or on one's own body filled with the bliss of the sell. Then, through one's own nectar, one becomes alive with the supreme bliss.

O gazelled eye ! One, verily by applying the performance of religious austerities, great bliss arises immediately, by which the essence is illumined.

By blocking all the flux of perception the Prana Shakti moves slowly upwards through the spinal cord. At that time, feeling the sensation of an ant crawling in the body, one experiences the supreme bliss.

One should throw the blissful mind into the fire (manipura chakra) in the middle of that fibre like lotus stalk (Sushumna) or into that which is only full of air (Anahata Chakra). Then one is united with the remembrance of bliss.

By the union with Shakti there is excitation and in the end, one is absorbed into Shakti (energy). That bliss of union which is said to be the nature of Brahaman , the expanding consciousness, that bliss is in reality one's own self.

O Queen of Gods ! The bliss of a woman is attained even in the absence 'of Shakti. By fully remembering and absorbing the mind in the experience of kissing, hugging and embracing, the bliss swells.

When great joy is obtained by any event like meeting with relatives, one should concentrate on that with one pointedness, until the mind becomes absorbed and the bliss ever arises.

If a person concentrates on eating and drinking and the happiness obtained by that joy of taste, from such contemplation of enjoyment arises the state of fullness, which then becomes supreme joy or bliss.

As a result of concentration on the pleasures of the senses, such as music or song, the Yogis enjoy similar happiness and pleasure in the same.

38

Thus, being absorbed in that the Yogi ascends beyond the mind and becomes one with that Supreme God.

Whenever there is satisfaction of mind and the mind is held there alone, the nature of supreme bliss manifests.

By entering that state preceding sleep, where the awareness of the outer world has faded, then the mind is absorbed in the threshlod state, by which the supreme goddess illumines.

By gazing on the space that appears variegated by the rays of the sun or an oil lamp, there the nature of one's essential self is illumined.

At the time of intuitive perception the attitude of Karankini, Krodhana, Bhairavi, Lelihanaya and Khechari are revealed, whereby the Supreme attainment manifests.

Seated on a soft seat, through one buttock, with hands and legs relaxed, at this time the mind becomes full of transcendence.

Sitting in a correct posture or position and curving the arms and hands into a circle, concentrate or fix the gaze inside this space. The mind becomes peaceful by this Laya.

One should steady the gaze without blinking on the gross form of any object. When the mind is transfixed and made supportless without any other thought or feeling, it at once acquires the state of Shiva or transcendence.

On placing the middle of the tongue in that which has been opened widely and throwing the conciousness in the middle, mentally repeating 'HA', the mind will be dissolved in tranquility.

While sitting or lying down, one should think of one's own body as being supportless or suspended in space. Then, in a moment the 'Samskaras' or thought constructs of the mind being reduced, it ceases to be a reservoir of old mental dispositions.

O Goddess ! As a result of slowly swinging or rocking the body, one attains a tranquil state of mind and floats into the stream of divine consciousness.

O Devi, on fixing the gaze continuously on the clear sky without blinking and with a steady awareness, at once the nature of Bhairava is achieved.

One should contemplate on the sky as the form of Bhairava until it is all absorbed in the forehead. Then all that space will be entered by the essence of light in the state of Bhairava.

On knowing a bit about duality, the outer light and darkness in the manifest world and so on, one who again experiences the infinite form of Bhairava procures illumination.

Like this, one should ever contemplate on the terrible darkness of night during the dark fortnight of the moon, if he desires to attain the form of Bhairava.

Similarly, while closing the eyes, one should contemplate on the profound darkness spreading in front as the form of Bhairava. Thus, he becomes one with that.

Whoever restrains even the same sense organ enters the one void without a second by this obstruction and there the Atma, or self, is illumined.

O Devi ! By recitation of Akaara 'A', in the absence of Bindu and Visarga, a great torrent of knowledge of the Supreme God, Parameshawara, at once arises.

When the mind is joined with the Visarga, at the end of the Visarga it is made supportless. In this way the mind is touched by the eternal Brahma, or the supreme consciousness.

When one concentrates on one's own self or soul in the form of unlimited space in all directions, the mind is suspended and Shakti in the form of consciousness is revealed in the form of one's own self or soul.

At first one should penetrate any limb of the body a little bit with a sharp, pointed needle or any other instrument. Then projecting the consciousness there, verily there is movement towards the pure nature of Bhairava.

Thus, by contemplating on the Antahkarana (inner space) or inner instrument of mind, and so on is non-existent within me, then, in the absence of Vikalpas or thought constructs, one becomes free from the Vikalpas.

Maya is the delusive principle residing in manifest existence, which cause name and limited activity. Thus, considering the nature or functions of the various elements, one realizes that he is not separate from the supreme reality.

When one observe the desires, which spring up in a flash, put an end to them. Then verily the mind will be absorbed in the very source from which they have arisen.

Thus, one should contemplate, when my desires do not produce knowledge, then What am I ? Indeed being absorbed in the essence I am, and identifying with that, one becomes that.

When desire or knowledge arises, one should fix the mind there, thinking that to be the very self. Making the mind absolutely one pointed in this way, he realizes the essence of the tattwas.

O Dear ! When you compared with absolute knowledge, all relative knowledge is without cause, and thus becomes baseless and deceptive. In reality, knowledge does not belong to any one person. Contemplating like this, one becomes Shiva.

Bhairava is of the nature of undifferentiated consciousness in all embodied forms. Therefore, those persons who contemplate on all creation pervaded by that consciousness, transcend relative existence.

When lust, anger, greed, delution, arrogance and jealousy are seen within, on fixing the mind completely on these, the underlying tattwa, or essence, alone remains.

Like Indrajal (illusion, illusive or imagined), the whole world is busy as a magic show or a painting. On ceding illusion and seeing all existence as transient, the happiness arises.

O Goddess ! The mind should not dwell on pain or pleasure, but the essence that remains in the middle (between pain and pleasure) should be known.

Abandoning consideration for one's own body, one should contemplate with a firm mind that, 'I am everywhere'. When this is seen by means of concentrated insight, one does not see another and thus becomes happy.

Contemplating on that special knowledge, i.e. the desires, exist not only within me but everywhere, one thus becomes all pervasive.

The subject and object conciousness is common to everybody. Yogis are especially alert regarding this relationship.

Contemplate on conciousness, such as one's own and even in another's body as well. Thus abandoning all physical expectation, one becomes all pervasive in the course of time.

O Gazelle-eyed ! Having free the mind of all supports, one should refrain from all the Vikalpas (thoughts, counter-thoughts, or options). Then, the self becomes one with the supreme God and the state of Bhairava achieved.

The Supreme God, who is omnipresent, omnicient and omnipotent, verily, I am lie and I have the same Shiva nature. Thus, contemplating with firm conviction, one becomes Shiva (Bhairava).

Just as waves arise from water, lames from lire and the light rays from the sun, similarly the waves of Bhairava, which produce the different emanations of the universe, are verily my source. So, the Universal waves is with us.

Whirling the body round and round rapidly, until it falls on the ground, makes the energy like commotion at once and become static. Due to sudden cessation the supreme state appears and thus Bhairava revealed.

On being powerless to perceive objects due to ignorance or wrong perception, if one is able to disintegrate the mind by absorbing it on the erroneous perception of objects, then at end of commotion brought about by that absorption, then the state of Bhairava achieved.

O Devi ! Listen, as I am saying you about this (mystic) tradition in its entirely. If the eyes are fixed in a steady gaze without blinking, Kaivalya (solitude, detachment, or isolation), which is the ultimate goal of Raja yoga, will arise immediately.

On closing or contracting the openings of the ears and also the lower opening (reproductive or excretory organs/parts) same as former, and then meditating or concentrating on the palace of Anahad (unstruck) sound within, one achieves the eternal Brahma.

On standing on a deep well or on a deep trough and looking steadily downward into the abyss, the mind becomes entirely free of Vikalpas (thoughts) and dissolution immediately reveals and thus the state of Bhairava achieved.

Wherever the mind (thoughts) flow or moves, supposing outwards or inwards, then there all pervasive state of Shiva will go.

Wherever the conciousness leads through the channel of the eyes, by contemplation on that object alone being of the same nature as that of the supreme, absorption of mind and the state of Poornatwa (the complete form) are experienced.

At the beginning and the end of sneezing, in terror, in sorrow or confusion, when fleeing from a battlefield, during keen curiosity, or at the onset or appeasement of hunger, that state is the external existence of Brahma.

When the mind leave aside i.e. all the
memorable objects and things of the
past, such as country or land, and
making the body supportless, then the
omnipresent and the mighty God, the
Bhairava, revealed.

O Goddess ! Momentarily casting the
gaze on some object and slowly
withdrawing it with the knowledge and
impression of that object, one becomes
the abode of the void.

That, instution which emerges from the
intense devotion of one who is
perfectly detached is known as the
Shakti of Shankara. By contemplating

regularly on that Shakti, God Shiva, Bhairava, revealed there.

When one perceives a paritcular object, vacuity is established regarding all other objects. Contemplating on that vacuity verily, even though the particular object is still known or perceived, the mind rests in tranquility.

What people of little understanding believe to be purity is neither pure nor impure to one who has experienced Shiva. The Nirvikalpa (freedom from Vikalpa), is the real purification by which one attains happiness.

The reality of Bhairava dwells everywhere, even in ordinary people. Thus, by contemplating, there is nothing other than him, when one attains the non-dual state of homogenous awareness.

One who makes no distinction between friend and foe, honour and dishonour, knowing Brahman to be full in itself all pervading, becomes supremely happy.

One should never think in terms of friendship or enmity. Being free from this idea of friend and foe, in between the Brahma Bhava, or nature of supreme conciousness blooms.

By contemplating on Bhairava as all
that which is void and cannot be
known, grasped or imagined, at the
end realization takes place.

Concentrating or fixing the mind in the
outer space, which is eternal, without
support, void, omnipresent and beyond
estimation or calculation, one enters
into the formless, unmanifest
dimension.

Wherever the mind dwells, casting that
aside that very moment, the mind

becomes supportless and free from disturbance.

The word Bhairava denotes the person who dispels all fear and terror, who howls and cries, who gives all, and who pervades the entire universe. The person who constantly repeats the word Bhairava becomes one with Shiva.

At the time of asserting, 'I am','this is mine', and so on, by inspired meditation on God, the highest reality, the mind becomes supportless.

Meditating every moment on the words like eternal, omnipresent, supportless, all-pervasive, master of the universe, one attains fulfillment in accordance with their meaning.

This world is illusory like a magic, devoid of any essence. What essence exists in magic? Being firmly convinced of this, one attains peace.

How can there be knowledge or activity of the changeless Atman, or self? All external objects are under the control of knowledge. Therefore, this world is void.

There is neither bondage nor liberation for me. These scare cowards and are the reflections or projections of the intellect, just as the sun is reflected in water.

All the doors of perception produce pain and pleasure through contact with the senses. Thus, casting aside the sensory objects and withdrawing the senses within, one abides in one's own self.

Knowledge or wisdom reveals all and the self of all is the revealer or knower. One should contemplate on the knowledge and the knower as being one and the same.

O Dear! When the mind, awareness, energy and individual self, this set of four dissolves, then the state of Bhairava revealed.

O Goddess! I have briefly told you more than one hundred and twelve ways whereby the mind is rendered still without any surge of thought, by knowing which people become wise.

One attains the state of Bhairava, if established even in one of these, one hundred and twelve dharanas, and by his speech one confers blessings or curses.

O Goddess! By virtue of even one of these Dharanas (beliefs), the Sadhaka becomes free from old age, attains immortality and endowed with Siddhis (success), such as Anima. He becomes the darling of all Yoginis and master of all Siddhas.

SHRI DEVI SAID :

O Great God! If this is the nature of the supreme reality, he is liberated while living and not affected by the activities of the world while active.

65

Thus, tell me in the established order, who would be invoked and what would be the invocation? Who is to be worshipped or meditated upon and who is to be gratified by that worship?

To whom should the invocations be made, to whom should oblations be offered during the sacrifice and how should these be done?

SHRI BHIRAVA SAID :

O Devi! These acts are verily the gross forms of worship.

Contemplate on the thought of being in the supreme consciousness again and again, this is also Japa (meditation or recitation). That self, which is spontaneously produced, is verily the soul of mantra. Japa is done like this.

When the intellect becomes steady, formless and without any support, meditation is verified. Imagination of the form of the divine with a body, eyes, mouth, hands, etc. is not meditation.

Offering of flowers, etc. is not Pooja or worship of God, but making one's mind steady in Mahakasha, the great void or space, and thoughtless in Nirvikalpa is worship indeed. From such reverence, dissolution of mind takes place.

By being established in any one of the practices described here, whatever experience is produced, develops clay by day until the state of absolute fullness or satisfaction is attained.

The real oblation is made when the elements and sense perceptions along with the mind are poured as oblation into the fire of the great void or space, i.e. Bhairava or Supreme conciousness, using the consiousness as a ladle.

O Parvati! Here the sacrifice characterized by bliss and satisfaction becomes the saviour of all by the destruction of all sins.

The greatest contemptation is that state where one is absorbed into the Shakti of Rudra. Otherwise how can there be any worship of that element and who is it dial is to be gratified?

One's own self is verily the all-pervasive bliss of freedom and the essence of conciousness. Absorption into that nature or form of one's own self is said to be the real bath or purification.

The oblations and the worshipper by which verily the transcendental reality is worshipped are all one and the same. What then is this worship?

Prana and Apana, having moved swiftly in a distinct direction, by the wish of Kundalini, that great Goddess stretches or elongates herself and becomes the supreme place of pilgrimage of both manifest and unmanifest.

One who pursues and abides in this sacrifice which is full of supreme bliss attains by the grace of that Goddess, the supreme state of Bhairava reaveled.

70

The breath is exhaled with the sound 'HA' and inhaled again with the sound 'SA'. Thus the individual always repeats this particular mantra Hamsa.

This Japa of Devi which was previously indicated, being repeated twenty one thousand six hundred times during the day and night, is easily available and difficult only for the ignorant.

O Goddess! This most excellent teaching, which is said to lead to the immortal state, should verily not be revealed to anybody.

71

These teachings should not be disclosed to other disciples, to those who are evil and cruel, or to those who have not surrendered to the feet of the Guru. They should only be revealed to advanced souls, who are self-controlled and whose minds are lice of Vikalpas.

Those devotees of the Guru, who are without the slighest doubt or hesitation having renounced son, wife, relatives, home, village, kingdom and country, should be accepted for initiation.

O Goddess! The worldly accoutrements are all temporary, but this supreme wealth is everlasting.

One may give up even one's Prana (life, energy), but this teaching which is the supreme nectar should never be given up.

SHRI DEVI SAID :

O God of Gods Shiva! I am now fully satisfied.

Today I have understood the quintessence of Rudrayamala Tantra and also from the innermost core of the heart of all the different Shaktis.

Thus saying, the Goddess being steeped in delight embraced Shiva.

Made in United States
Orlando, FL
18 November 2022